BOOKS BY JOHN HOLLANDER

Poetry

Tesserae and Other Poems   1993
Selected Poetry   1993
Harp Lake   1988
In Time and Place   1986
Powers of Thirteen   1983
Blue Wine and Other Poems   1979
Spectral Emanations: New and Selected Poems   1978
Reflections on Espionage   1976
Tales Told of the Fathers   1975
The Head of the Bed   1974
Town and Country Matters   1972
The Night Mirror   1971
Types of Shape   1969
Visions from the Ramble   1965
Movie-Going   1962
A Crackling of Thorns   1958

Criticism

Rhyme's Reason   1981
    A Guide to English Verse
The Figure of Echo   1981
    A Mode of Allusion in Milton and After
Vision and Resonance   1975
    Two Senses of Poetic Form
The Untuning of the Sky   1961
    Ideas of Music in English Poetry 1500–1700

For Children

The Immense Parade on Supererogation Day
    and What Happened to It   1972
The Quest of the Gole   1966

TESSERAE

& OTHER POEMS

TESSERAE
& OTHER POEMS
BY JOHN HOLLANDER

Alfred A Knopf   New York 1995

ACKNOWLEDGMENTS:

Antaeus: from "Tesserae" ("Quatrains of Doubt and Death")
Forward: from "Tesserae" ("Poetishe Fersen")
Grand Street: from "Tesserae" ("Autumn Quatrains")
Kenyon Review: from "Tesserae" ("Final Arrangements")
London Review of Books: "The Week's Events," "The Art of Fiction"
Midstream: "Making Nothing Happen"
The Nation: "From Out of the Black," "Into the Black"
The New Criterion: "Cissy's Song"
The New Republic: "An Old-Fashioned Song," "Colored Illustration, Tipped In,"
    "Edward Hopper's Seven A.M.," "The See Saw"
The New Yorker: from "Tesserae" ("Days of Summer"), "Behind the Beaux-Arts"
New York Review of Books: "An Old Counting Game"
Paris Review: from "Tesserae" ("At the Follies"), "Early Inscription,"
    "Variations on a Fragment by Trumbull Stickney," "A Line from Dubellay"
Quarterly West: "February Madrigal"
Raritan: From "Tesserae" ("Below the Belt," When Spring Comes Round Again,"
    "Bits and Piece Work"), "Ballad for an Old Tune, No Refrain"
Salmagundi: "Air for the Musette," "Perseus Holds Medusa's Head Aloft"
Southwest Review: "On North Rock"
Tel Aviv Review: "An Old Counting-Game"
Western Humanities Review: "Green-Shadowed Rocks"
The Yale Review: "River Remembered"

"10/28/29," and "Song at the End of a Meal" originally published in *Some Fugitives Take Cover*, privately printed, copyright © 1988 by John Hollander.
"Now and Then" originally published in *The State of the Language*, edited by Ricks and Michaels, University of California Press, 1990

Library of Congress Cataloging-in-Publication Data

Hollander, John.
    Tesserae:and other poems / by John Hollander.—1st ed.
        p.   cm.
    ISBN 0-679-76200-0
    I. Title.
PS3515.03485T46   1993   92-54792
811'.54—dc20   CIP

For Sandy McClatchy

CONTENTS

I

Notes on some of the poems will be found on page 87

AN OLD-FASHIONED SONG

(Nous n'irons plus au bois)

No more walks in the wood:
The trees have all been cut
Down, and where once they stood
Not even a wagon rut
Appears along the path
Low brush is taking over.

No more walks in the wood;
This is the aftermath
Of afternoons in the clover
Fields where we once made love
Then wandered home together
Where the trees arched above,
Where we made our own weather
When branches were the sky.
Now they are gone for good,
And you, for ill, and I
Am only a passer-by.

We and the trees and the way
Back from the fields of play
Lasted as long as we could.
No more walks in the wood.

AN OLD COUNTING-GAME

What's all this fuss about 1? One?
Once you are dead, Eternity's begun.

What do they say about 2? Two?
Tomb and its Emptiness are far too few.

What's the real point about 3? Three:
The Real, the Unreal, and their dreamer, Me.

There's 4: explain it to me. Four
Form my extremities, one heart their core.

I want to know about 5 then, Five:
Fie, vain, literal digits! Bytes now thrive.

How is poor 6 now feeling? Six?
Sick still at closing time, his feet are bricks.

More about famous 7? Seven?
Sev—enough now of that Highest Heaven.

What of the 8 beyond that? Eight
Ate for's and to's, left nothing on his plate.

Gestation aside, then, 9: Nine?
Nigh nowhere, the high home-run scorned the line.

I still forget what 10 meant. Ten?
Tenderly awkward, as we all were then.

SONG AT THE END OF A MEAL

The kid was already noxious carrion
That poisoned our kitty when she lunched on it;
The cat clawed at the neighbor's dog who bit
At her tail—infection left the dog undone,
But not before he snapped a stick in two
That fell across his flanks as if to beat
The beast as with a will of its own; the heat
Of a fire that burned the stick was made to rue
The day on which it was born, as half the stick
Flew through the air and knocked its flames apart.
(The fire meanwhile vaporized the wet heart
Of the water that sought to quench it, that made sick
The ox that sought to drink it, who in turn
Brought down with nasty anthrax the butcher who would
Have slaughtered him; that butcher pierced the hood
Of the Angel of Death, from whom we all must learn.)
But how did that dark Angel turn his wrath upon
His would-be punisher, Blessed be He, the Holy One?

MAKING NOTHING HAPPEN

Poetry makes nothing happen   W. H. AUDEN

Before there could be nothing, there were too,
Too many somethings, all abuzz: *tohu*
Scrapping with *bohu*; pain and desire, delight
And fear; a whorl of knowings; dim and bright
Suspended in a universal blanc-
Mange. She could not allow this to go on.
She said, *Let there be night* and there was night,
Intensest night, within which Nothing might
Be seen emerging from its ruined tomb;
Making itself a kind of spaceless room;
Setting its engines of denial stirring;
And then, quite irreversibly, occurring.
Nothing had, finally, happened. In future, then,
Something would never be the same again.

BEHIND THE BEAUX-ARTS

Framing my windows on the outside of the building are:
A pediment hanging in the way of height; two engaged
Columns of a mixed order; beneath them a corbelled sill.

How splendid they seem from the street below! How important
The room that gazes out of these windows, not through but past
All the obviating fussiness of blocked masonry

(For any glance outside the windows flies by the columns,
Disdaining the peaked shawl of the sandstone to claim only
The bright prize of morning sunlight reflected in windows
Opposite, framed in the shadows of their oblong sockets).

And what does the room know of her outward bravery and
Its hard adornment? She would seem to grasp more of herself,
Her place within, air, dust, and light, the strange ways of her space—

Allowing itself to be occupied, for instance, by
A flat yellow trapezoid of sunlight lying along
The floor, the bed, the chair, the table, falling all over
Themselves to touch the hem of that visiting radiance.

The room would believe herself to be just so filled, just so
Emptied. But about the carved portals of her gaze she does
Not have the airiest idea, the dustiest guesses.

Then do not liken our eyes, straining for their own visions
Of gold, to our windows peering out from under portals:
If they are indeed windows, why, rip them out of their frames!

Let the high, mindless wind howl through the whole chamber behind,

That the mind, in its wisdom without eyes, may truly see.

COLORED ILLUSTRATION, TIPPED-IN

A sun, slipping under
The rim of visibility, unfurled
That flagrant bunting of his half-surrender,
Half-promise of returning to the world.

And what of the water?
—The sea composed herself into a scene
Knowing what old illuminations taught her:
That only gold could highlight ultramarine.

There, the horizon,
So far and linear and purified
Of middle distance and the lively poison
Of interestingness—from it, all have died.

What of this island,
Clouded, condensed and battered by the sea?
Arising amidst cliffs, a craggy highland
Makes rocky waves and breaking land agree.

What of the castle
Rising above it on the nearer shore,
Walled-in and walling out, in that most facile
Of concrete versions of the either/or?

(Yes, but that casement
In the near parapet, above the berm,
Propounds, though at the price of some defacement
Of all that wall, a kind of middle term.)

What of the tower,
Built recently by a demented king
As in some sort of show of no real power,
Dark-house, unbeaconing, unbeckoning?

What of the chamber
Below, attended by a deaf-mute page?
A room in which to dream, and half-remember
What once had been one in another age.

And what of the mirror
So proud to have composed a royal face
Upon it?—with the princess wandering here or
There in the castle, it stands in blank disgrace.

But that dark puddle
Of ink spilled on the floor returns the light
Of sunset that, in the inverted muddle
It makes of things, reads as red dawn of night;

And the whole picture:
Puddle invisible in such small scale
We turn from its coated stock to a rough texture,
The paper of a new page, of a new tale.

EDWARD HOPPER'S SEVEN A.M. (1948)

The morning seems to have no light to spare
For these close, silent, neighboring, dark trees,
But too much brightness, in low-lying glare,
For middling truths, such as whose premises
These are, and why just here, and what we might
Expect to make of a shop-window shelf
Displaying last year's styles of dark and light?
Here at this moment, morning is most itself,
Before the geometric shadows, more
Substantial almost than what casts them, pale
Into whatever later light will be.
What happens here? What is the sort of store
Whose windows frame such generality?
Meaning is up for grabs, but not for sale.

THE TESSERAE (I)

1

Night beside me, I turn from her toward day,
Cloyed with the stillness of our common clay,
      And twitted in the morning by the birds
For not delighting in their brightened gray.

2

Two radioed fiddles thread their minor thirds
Among the unmeaning chirpings of the birds;
      In silent light, language is not yet up
And about: my late, light dreams are all of words.

3

This dream was broken by my opening eyes:
Flowers in pots . . . among them, butterflies
      Tiny, and like in flowers in color, swarm
Before resemblance in the daylight dies.

4

Young, in the afternoon, I'd wandered free
In the lost places I'd once thought to flee;
      The Old Man of the Morning, now, I'm found
Silent beside the loudly sounding sea.

5

The river's literal rustlings never roar
At its attentive banks—thus all the more
      Strange, the sea's listening restlessness, and all
That thundering along the stone-deaf shore.

6

"The sun sees everything: we have our sight
Only because of its all-seeing light."
        —Old pictures of Apollo labelled thus
Appall the wisdom of all-knowing Night.

7

June morning. High, young light in its own way
Says what the old Greek Thales had to say
        About the age of Chaos and Old Night:
"Old" Night is older than—by just a—Day.

8

The ardent hands of sunlight in the morning
Love the cool body of the land, but scorning
        Defacements of its personality,
Can get turned off with just a touch of warning.

9

My mind takes root in daylight, where I see
The meditative shore absorbed in sea
        And thoughts of sea, and all that sea had thought
Of sky. I stand like an inverted tree.

10

Bright morning on the shadowy meadow turned
From cool truth into glaring fact. We yearned
        For trope: noon's zealous flames of inquisition
Shed too much light and left no stone unburned.

11

July. There's "liquid" melody, the tune
Of treachery: the hidden, waiting moon
  Now pours into the porches of my ear
Birdsong from somewhere in the afternoon.

12

The flaming *mullah* in his house of lead
Raves fruitlessly among the faithful dead.
  The Persian melon cooling in the shade
Keeps summer's wisdom in its sleeping head.

13

One of the old gods, golden and adored
Whose wordless service was its own reward
  Once whispered in the shade toward which I turned
From where the lion of the sunlight roared.

14

Along the margin of the margin lies
The trembling threshold, set between the wise
  And probing questions of the afternoon
And indoor answers where the daylight dies.

15

We bookworms of the Tale of Life, alas,
Consume each day what will have come to pass,
  While the great Loafer, vagrant, beds him down
On annual leavings of the summer's grass.

16

July winds up its business there in town.
The vacancies of avenues will crown
  The coming and majestic month of fire
In which the summer's engines will wind down.

17

The widened freeway bound in traffic burning
In heat of flight or motionless, unlearning
  Ever of where roads lead. Eternity?
Oh yes: it's a long lane that has no turning.

18

The city's forest of despairs . . . to flee
Its fires of—alas, yes—humanity,
  Homesick and yet sick of homecomings
I took to the woods: they did not take to me.

19

Tinged with false promise, edged with polychrome,
The sunset's red drips up along its dome;
  Tuning the corded jibsheet to the strum
Of evening air we make a run for home.

20

The shadows that these pots cast on the bright
Surfaces of adjacent ones make light
  Of weight, and darken only that they may
Pretend to depth with all their weightless might.

21

Twilight and meaning, darkness and rising hope
Stretched out across my path a twisted rope.
        Last night, in simple truth, I fell asleep.
Today I trip over last evening's trope.

22

The grain all gathered, and the aftermath
All sifted, and the threshing-out of wrath
        Complete, we're left with nothing more to glean
Than these leaves fallen on our homeward path.

23

Mingling with the steadier stuff that spills
Down from the fallen shadows of the hills,
        From vanished cottage chimneys risen smoke
Assents to what the coming darkness wills.

24

A shriek, from somewhere in the August night,
Pierces me, of some animal in fright
        Or in the cruel and warm embrace of death
That cries out just as fiercely in delight.

25

Night on the bay: the sound of daylight's daughter
When grabbed at by the abundant hands of water
        (The singularity of the low moon
Laughing at the redundant waves that caught her.)

26

The self-sustaining ardor of a bright
Candle-flame, steady in this windless night,
  Reflected in its tiny cup of oil:
It draws from its own image heat and light.

27

However fragile, callow and uncouth,
Brazen and shy, at least once, in her youth,
  Everyone standing free of clothes before
Her pensive mirror will look just like Truth.

28

The moon shone in my cup of thought to pour
Therein her lewd light and its darker lore;
  I was reminded by the glistening brim
Of lives I'd somehow led not long before.

29

In silence that serves further to entrance her
Body's feeling of itself, a dancer
  Moving without a music: so the thought
Of loss whirls by—a question. Or an answer?

30

Perched on the branches of this aging tree
As in Freud's sketch of Wolf-Man's dream, I see
  Holes in the foliage, made of present sky,
Where what is missing gazes absently.

31

Standing in total darkness, like a stone,
And seeing nothing—it is then I've known
      With knowing Wittgenstein the unboundedness
Of visions's field in which we are alone.

II

BALLAD FOR AN OLD TUNE, NO REFRAIN

It was down in Jo's apartment
  On a corner of Gramercy Park
They were lighting up the street-lamps
  But inside it was dark.

On the floor by the piano
  Lay a square of yellow light
Led in through the square of the window
  From the inquisitive night.

Thrown over the piano
  Lay a blood-red Paisley shawl;
Dimly lit, its familiar pattern
  Could hardly be read at all.

The keys of the piano
  Shone black and bluish-white:
Jo was playing chains of ninth-chords
  To someone out of sight.

An indiscernible picture
  On the wall above a shelf
In the bedroom had been yearning
  For a shadow of itself,

Looked out there for a shadow
  It might have been able to cast
On a square of light from the window
  But saw nothing present or past;

Saw nothing, heard only an echo
  Of a voice it never possessed
While Jo hummed on in the next room
  A song whose words were at rest

(The music of meditation
  Whose ardor will never scorch—
The light of a blue-note just can't
  Hold a candle to a torch)

But would have gone "*Lover come find me,*
  I'm waiting here all alone"
—Then she modulated and lowered
  The melody by a tone:

Lover, come find where my heart is
  Lover, I've waited too long—"
She spoke from her heart in the ninth-chords
  But the words were just words of a song

The echo that night returned her
  "*Lover come home to me*"
Was drained of what we'd call meaning
  And empty of irony:

She hears a noise from her bedroom
  Obscuring what she half-sings
Like a rat running over a table
  Covered with fabric and things,

Like a shuffle and cough and rustle
  That a shadow of terror had made
Like what could be read of an image
  If an image could cast a shade.

She starts up and runs to the bedroom
  And switches on the light
Unveiling a silent picture
  Painted in strokes of fright:

She stands, caught in the grasp of
    The ceiling-light's sudden display,
Gazing with flattened perspective
    At her dresser in disarray,

And there by her dresser a figure
    Smelly, brutal and rough,
We are forced to acknowledge as human
    Was rifling through her stuff.

As if the intruder had vanished,
    She and her fear were alone
Her pounding heart told her nothing:
    There was nothing to know or be known.

But then, from an unsilenced pistol,
    Information of a sort:
She half-heard the dreadful message
    Encoded in its report

With never a flash of knowledge,
    The effortless work on the part
Of a .357 Magnum
    Did great things to her heart.

She fell to a square of yellow
    Throw-rug on the floor
As if such echoes of pattern
    Could matter any more.

Her blood leaked out on the carpet,
    For her heart had started to die,
Her life despairingly left her
    And did itself in thereby.

Her blood leaked out on the carpet
Cup by cup, not drop by drop;
Her life despairingly left her.
Period—*Punkt*—Full stop.

So the Urban Ordinary
With perhaps one final wail
Punctuates stanzas and gives a
Pointless end to a tale.

BREAD-AND-BUTTER!

Walking together for so many years
They could hold hand in hand and still avoid
What a jackhammer or a dog had done
To or on the sidewalk—such was the supple
Touch they kept in, such the ample closeness
That marked their every way of walking by
The way (and sitting in their house and lying
Down and rising up, for all that, as well)

And what they would pass by on either side—
On each one's side—dissolved into the air,
The general air, of the phase or stage of things
They and their local walk were moving through
Until it seemed that they could not be said
To share the walk they took so much as that
The walk itself, a tall, responsible
Adult, went between them, holding both their hands

Until they happened on the unexpected
Obstacle—and whether it had leapt up
As an expanded stumbling-block too massy
And oddly-formed merely to trip over,
Or cried out silently and suddenly
In an abyss, all hands parted, they passed

He to the left	She rightward then with *Bread*
Around it, saying *Bread*	*And Butter!* said
And Butter! out	Of touch and loss of touch;
Of phase and finally out	Of childhood that
Of contact with	Had lingered with her long,
Some mass of palpable,	The phrase she spoke
Immediate	Itself spoke; but by then
Souvenir then, and yet	The time for hands
Avoiding that	Laughingly to rejoin

Abyss of memory
   The phrase's taste
Upon his uttering tongue
   Could open up.
By then his hands no more
   Could even feel
Anticipations of
   A touch regained;
These two could not be read
   As from above,
Say, as "the two of them":
   Looking across
The separation now
   Had made no sense
For some time now in fact
   Or fiction too.
Only our love of closures
   Keeps us longing
For bridges, tunnels, hands
   But there was no
Common pathway ahead
   no *You that way*...
Ending some comedy
   as holding out
Against time, holding out
   Both hands and hope

Was gone. The gap
   Between them now was all
The making of
   Their walk itself; the way
She took, the way
   She had been taking now
Was not just hers,
   Let alone part of theirs,
But merely all
   The way there was. The cut
Lines on the sidewalk
   Between the concrete squares
And which the games
   Of childhood cut so deep
Were not the same
   There on the other side.
Only our lust
   For soft connections still
Keeps us in quest
   Of some clear syntax here.
Both, neither, said:
   We this way—a confirmed
Deferral or
   Contemporary sort
Of difference
   As if it were a word

Enough, though, of such literal narratives:
They had buttered their bread and eaten it.
Now distances shall not allow our straining
Eyes to track their faint courses any more
Where only the limitations of some page
Had made their ways seem to run parallel,
And only death would lay them lower than
The concrete actualities they walked
And leave them holding hands again with dust.

10/28/29

I THE DAY ITSELF SPEAKS

The day of my birth glares at me
From out of the black-framed front page
Of a newspaper of that date.
Standing on the floor, tilted up
Against low bookshelves and blocking
Easy access to what volumes
Are there behind it, tilted up
In the poor light across the room,
The staring glass reflects a low
Ceiling and casts the page, headlines
And all, into a grayish blank,
Save for *"The New York Times"* in that
Old, still assuring, (but of what?)
Black letter. What has it to say
For itself, late in the lost day?
—"Don't look at me like that, for I
Promised you only that you'd die."

2   GREETINGS

Time tips over Libra's
Pan, and now our Day drops
Just into the pincers
Of the Scorpion. *Well,*
Many happy returns
(And, given what you have
Given, there had better
Be something returned: the
Bread of all your days cast
Upon the receding
Waters must come back as
Something more than a mere
Cake) *And may you have a*
Good many more (Fat Chance!)
Fat? I suppose she is;

Not the meagre whore that
Fortune used to be when
Luck was understood to
Be inconstant. Now we
Know her, fat and earnest,
To invest herself more
Wisely, and to fold her
Hand before drawing more
Cards to a sure loser.
Perish the day wherein
I was born. (*Don't worry:*
Like all our other days
It went its way at once.)

FROM OUT OF THE BLACK

That afternoon, the world began to hum
With the low moan of everything that mattered.
In the long darkness that a flash had shattered
We waited numbly for the crash to come:
Such sudden light could not illuminate
An after-dark too easy to take lightly,
Memory unknowing what now to await.
In silent white that struck my eyesight dumb,
The winding sheet of lightning wrapped me tightly.
Having retired into silence lately
The thunder rumbled now, till its pogrom
Erupted, and the villages of light
Trembled in terror; strong, I bowed down greatly;
I went mourning all the day long, like Night.

INTO THE BLACK

I was brought forth abroad at night, but not
To tally stars, consider the constellations
Or make the endless, pebbled calculations
Of every point and every half-seen spot;
But, looking up toward what had once been heaven.
To number and tell the spreading fields of dark,
Unharvestable, by which I would mark
The fate of my descendants six or seven
Generations hence, when grains of light
Ablaze in the dark ground of futuring sky
No longer come to life, no longer die
In their own fruitfulness: I have been sent
To found the new house of diminishment,
My growing tribe of emptiness and night.

Constant only in her grim
Way—as to waters that adore
Her, the moon's high face slides from prim
Crescent to heavenly queen and whore,
She was my fancy, I her whim.
Behind the veils of light she wore
Her clear, unclouded voice said "Trim
The lamp, and lock the cellar door"
Which I did, till my sight, grown dim,
Could not admire her any more.
I'd nothing to protect her slim,
No longer lambent, memory for,
No pools of dream in which to swim
Where she was someone of the shore.

THE TESSERAE (II)

32

Dusty leaves cast their shadows, and the bee,
That ancient prophetess, now wordlessly
    Buzzing of the wild wilderness, believes
These shadows cast by what will come to be.

33

Warm in the summer autumn fields grew cold;
We had been young then, then we would be old
    And thinking of the days that are no more
Than long past fallen leaves, and all their mold.

34

The full, ripe silence where the grain was sown
The lingering sigh of tall grass lately mown,
    Rise from these tedious, ordinary fields:
Don't draw on outline, but take note of tone.

35

The day of the long days has shed its noon,
Lain nakedly, and now awaits the moon,
    Donning the orange veil that sunset draws
Across what will be long ago too soon.

36

August remembered autumn, but not old
December, as its shortening days unrolled.
    Heat waved away, in summery dismissal
The winter's now-long-buried pot of cold.

37

Field; the late harvest standing still in sheaves:
Is it the rising of the wind that grieves
      My forest self, *mon* moi *longue d'Octobre*
Who sang before the falling of the leaves?

38

From an Old Song: "Among these laughing girls
In high sunlight, below her chestnut curls
      Tears rain from clouds behind her glistening eyes—
Not as in moonlight, when her tears are pearls."

39

Cadences of familiar songs Can lie
In hiding here Where fields and open sky
      Declaim In prose, unchanted, clear, The texts
Left high and dry When the fall wind swept by.

40

"*Ist Sommer? Sommer* war," wrote Paul Celan.
Imperfect autumn lingers, and so on
      And so forth while we pause as the last song
Of one lost summer swims by like a swan.

41

A *Liebhaber* of possibilities,
A connoisseur of loss, I drink the lees
      Of weakened vintages toward sundown, when
The sunlight gleams among the fallen trees.

42

At length, the hill of thought was undermined
By pain, tunneling through its hard and blind
    Rock, into which runs our advancing train,
Leaving the plain of fancies far behind.

43

Plucking and gathering still plant the seeds
Of folly: at the site of our misdeeds
    Of fruitless toil eked out with inattention
Earth laughs in flowers what she weeps in weeds.

44

Ah, for her I lost! for me whom I gave
Away to nothing! for all I could not save!
    The raving wind disperses in the oaks.
Light grieving slumps into a heavy grave.

45

Past sorrows—those our present joys embrace
In gentle mastery—will not displace
    The present sorrows for past joys, which meet
Half in shadow, face-to-averted-face.

46

Past, Absent and Future all unfold
Before our present eyes, high in the cold
    Height of a hill in 1953.
We had been young then, then we would grow old.

47

No nova flaring in November, less
And less renewal as the trees undress:
  We shiver down past mere noon and its non-
Age, and its hopeless whiffs of agelessness.

48

Blood's shadow lay beneath the light green shade
The chestnut branches by the meadow made.
  The field of beets became a battlefield,
The plough's fair share fell to another blade.

49

Stanzas and cameras, as well as dark
Rooms in mean cottages and brightened, stark
  Offices alike are merely spaces
Until the ghosts of Place have left their mark.

50

Autumn's brood stripped by late November's rude
Whips, our decaying health last year renewed
  Our well-known bodies' growing oddness, the
Stupidity of our decrepitude.

51

Above my dimmed eyes, the barn owl, below
The shivering mouse, and then—and so we go.
  The dark point of this nocturne's both what I
Believe I see and what I know I know.

52

It was the gray sidewalks which taught my feet
The truth of their particular concrete:
  All? not this general Being of the land;
The *Way?* not through the fields, but up the street.

53

A horse-and-buggy's slow to understand
The way of the road, the vastness of the land;
  To get across the heights, the breadths, I ride
The kind of carriage called a four-in-hand.

54

The years of childhood days—extended fears,
Joys and anticipations: time and tears
  Contract their terms, which, in the Psalmist' phrase
Have withered to the brief days of our years.

55

That bright, young person that I was, all prim
Exuberance, safe wonder, bridled vim:
  Ingrate! He never gave a damn for me.
I weep for what I could have done for him.

56

Shining in sunlight through the winter trees
These little brooks appear now as they freeze,
  At liberty to glitter, at long last
Recovered from fluidity's disease.

57

January. Epipromethean? or
Just plain two-faced? Here standing at the door
    Of the year, staring both in and out, he knows
What lies before him is what has gone before.

58

All our poor works of light come down to viewing
That deed of darkness to be our undoing,
    A cold and loveless act of quick uncoupling,
Counter-clockwise, a sort of last unscrewing.

59

Our first, misshapen version had two faces,
His, hers looked out at paradisal places—
    So goes the *midrash*—till the maker struck
Apart that form, and put us through our paces.

60

Imprisoned in the way our bodies fit
Together, we work out with straining wit
    Till yet more ageing breaks those lovely fetters.
Are we redeeming time by doing it?

61

The Talmud says *"What's mine is yours, yours, mine"*
Is a fool's paradox—lovers combine,
    In bed, folly and wisdom, dipping the bread
Of each of them each in the other's wine.

62

His mental being in her bodily
One: each is the other's property.
  And where they are becomes their everywhere;
Each there is here, just suited to a *t*.

63

Then repossessed of selves, drunk on their wine
Pressed from distrust, in re the iron line
  That now divides them, each may truly say
"What's mine of it is yours, what yours, is mine."

64

(Make up a sad old joke:) "I wonder who's
Kissing her now?" *Her* Now? *Inside her shoes?*
  Her shirt? Her pants? Her bonnet? Where's her Now?
Next to her Then, Fool! You had all the clues.

65

A sprightly pinnace, rigged for sport, a fine
Erotic frigate of a new design,
  Are intermittent fictions in the wake
Of that commanding flagship-of-the-line.

66

The pleasures of the moment now must cede
Their throne to awesome word and lawful deed:
  Stern Juno keeps her Jupiter in shape;
Hebe takes back the cup from Ganymede.

67

The auspex now looked downward—while, above,
The deadly hawk and the infected dove
    Fluttered and soared—and then exhorted us,
For love of safety, to make war, not love.

68

The marriage wakened by the blast of horns,
The rosy ambush bristling with the thorns
    Of falsehood, hidden by night's shading strokes
That noon erases and that noone mourns.

69

But he who bedded down with grief and strife
And he who took felicity to wife,
    Alike are buried where the laureate earth
Hums elegies and lies about each life.

70

The little foxes of desire may cry
Out for their bits of how and what and why.
    We are like hedgehogs of the heavy heart:
The one big thing we know is that we'll die.

III

PERSEUS HOLDS MEDUSA'S HEAD ALOFT

Shrieking, is she in horror of her own hard pain
Or of the power of her petrifying gaze
Itself, astonishing, and of the pain new rock
Loses at its moment of birth? Or do her snakes,
Twisting, hurt her, mirroring her heart with a twist
Of imaging? Her heart was in her hair, her tongue
Was in her gaze, her cunt itself was stone always
Impenetrable, long before the sightless eyes
Had raked across the untopped tower of her body
Turning the rest to insufficiently abstract
Limestone. *Athena's gain is empty terror's loss,*
The inmost truths of stone lie riddled and concealed,
And thus that hard gaze ends up set in the hard boss
Of the unmothered virgin, gray-eyed Wisdom's shield.

CISSY'S SONG

The child writes her verses. Bookish snow
Falling beyond her windowpane
Dances elusively: dropping rain
In remembered summer of short ago
Played no descending games, and so
She scribbles away as much for the sake
Of remembered cadence, as for the ache
Of seeing one last falling leaf
Summer had held in unyielding fief,
A motif she will take:
"One last flake that refuses to linger
Pirouettes down on my outstretched finger."

Again she picks up her pen. The snow
Inscribed behind her windowpane
Dances allusively: winter's reign
Over remembrances cannot slow
The backward-running streams that flow
Up from the brimming past to creep
Into the present, where from deep
In their undreaming sleep, they make
Figures of innocence jingle and shake
And leave in their wake
One last leaf
        It refuses to linger,
And pirouettes down on her outstretched finger.

She turns to her desk, at a time of no
Snow: summoned up on her windowpane,
Returning in moments of refrain,
As if with her breath, words come and go
With just enough childish warmth to break
The cold white heart of a frozen lake
Her thoughts are lost in the cold of time
But two last lines, glittering with rime
Fifty years afterward startle awake
One last flake,
One last flake that refuses to linger
Pirouettes down on my outstretched finger.

GREEN-SHADOWED ROCKS

The truth of these moss-covered rocks, uncracked
By quarrying of time, lies in the fact
Of how they are, here, now, under his eyes
Which have been scanning X and Y, likewise
Reading about in *alpha* yesterday,
Wondering what in *beta* underlay
The harder parts of *gamma*, and thereby
Remembering a long-forgotten *xi*
While the wind played it back. It's growing late,
And just because he'll not appropriate
Part of the given, he returns them to
Nature, warmed by the handling of his few
Thoughts, daubed with the colors of allusion
Henceforth now part of them. Not the intrusion
Of knowledge upon rock. Not unkicked stone
Refuting something about being known
As simply Being. But the truth of rock
(Which only new redaubing can unlock).

FAR AWAY

We say "far away"; the Zulu has a word for it which means, in our sentence form, "There where someone cries out: 'O mother, I am lost'." The Fuegian soars above our analytic wisdom with a seven-syllabled word whose precise meaning is, "They stare at one another, each waiting for the other to volunteer to do what both wish, but are not able to do."

MARTIN BUBER, *I and Thou,*

TR. R. G. SMITH

It can't be time to reach out for her yet
    Because, before my hand could get
        Near
Enough to touch hers, it might disappear
(The hand, that is) or else, that part of her
    —"Of hand, of lip, of foot, of eye,
        Of brow," or thigh
        Or what thigh might defer—
The hand sought touch with would itself dissolve
    Into thick air. Then, too, that might involve
—Moving toward her in any way,
That is—one more loss at too great a price to pay:
    That distance which has taken place between
        Us both, I mean—
    Distance itself would vanish there
Into suspension in the ambient air.

That would be mad:
The thought of abandoning what we had—
Your firm *there* and my sturdy *here*—
Fills me with fear.
And what in each of us welcomes the other's touch
Is such
As to ordain that what is true
Of, for, and to, me goes as well for you.
Thus seven English syllables embrace
Each of us in our sovereignty of place,
Of *he* and *she*:
(The word is "too-close-and-we'd-not-be-we").
More deeply then than any kiss
We both acknowledge this
In our paralysis
To terminate which then would disavow
The faith we both keep now,
As distant as a sparrow and a star.
So here we are.

EARLY INSCRIPTION

EIDLLA EW [DNA?] NROBLLA ERAEW

[NIEMAND'S TRANSLATION: *We are all born and we all die*]

(NIMMERWAHR, 1868)   Niemand's suggested emendation, as well as his translation based on it, will plainly not do; among other things, the pure uninterpretability of the text, which alone constitutes its significance, is thereby beclouded.

(SCHWARTZWEISS, 1869)   Significance, indeed! "Sing if"-icance, only an easy transposition away, puts Nimmerwahr's whole flimsy matter more accurately. Mere lyrical hypothesis gets us nowhere.

(NIRGENDSWO, 1869)   The text is quite clear, and if seemingly "uninterpretable" (thus Nimmerwahr!), only because it is merely so much a commonplace as to be trivial. Niemand's conjecture is, of course, quite sound.

(STILLSCHWEIGEND, 1870)   Sound? *Sound*!!!??? A ridiculous suggestion, all the more dangerous in that it invites the ill-considered judgment to agree with the reductively positive Schwartzweiss, who is, as always, incapable of grasping crucial nuance.

(LINDSAY-WOLSEY, 1902)   There is something uncanny about Niemand's suggested syllable, which represents, after all, the only intelligible morpheme in the inscription; it is, in the old Eastwest dialect, the word for "life." Niemand of course knew nothing of this, and his suggestion is as worthless as is the controversy it has elicited. Still, the very fact that he should have introduced it, sheds some ironic light not on the "meaning" of the text but on the meaning of the conditions generating its mode of reception.

(QUACKENBUSH, 1973)   The very power of this particular fragment to elicit such particularly heavy and humorless debate from nineteenth-century German scholars usually known for their light-handedness and grace in controversy is in some way a function of the resonance of its assertion, particularly in view of the fact that it is now believed to be impossible to assert just what that assertion might be. I am reminded of how . . .

(BERTOLDO, 1974)   Quackenbush leads us—ha! ha!—into a quackmire. The text says what it says; the English translation from Niemand will do as well as any.

(PETERSCHREIER, 1988)   Merely to quote this sentiment [Niemand's "We are all born and we all die." Ed.] is outrageous. "*We*"??? This means, as usual, humans, and the whole utterance manifests the worst sort of species-ism. The assertion is an affront to other species *who can't be said to "know" that they will die.* It is a slippery slope from boasting of the ultimate human knowledge to asserting, vilely, mankind's hegemony over "the garden of Creation."

(VRUN-LÜGNER, 1990)   As we now know, Niemand went wrong in not realizing that the inscription falls into two parts that are actually in two different dialects; EIDLLA EW is in the lingua franca of the North, and NROBLLA ERAEW in the form used for inscriptions in the South. Whatever the words may mean, each "half" is a paraphrase of the other. Each says the same thing. Whether, at some other level, Niemand's erroneous translation might be considered a tautology is not for us to consider.

THE WEEK'S EVENTS

She said, affably, "Calm next Mahnday,"
Indicating that his pants would be ready by then.
But nonetheless unwittingly invoking a mysterious occasion,
Which, on ultimate reflection, appeared to be a sort
Of centennial celebration for the author of *Joseph and His Brothers*
And other works, even as it eventually turned out not to be.

"Let's have lunch on Tuesday," suggested Dubble-Barrell (he
Pronounced it "Jewsday", as if there had been inserted into the
    medieval calendar
Another liturgical day, devoted to violent expressions of rage
Against an unfortunate race, ungracious
In its refusals of redemption, tiresome in its endless
Ability to elicit persecution from the peoples of the West and
    elsewhere).

Brenda-Sue yawned; and—in the modern manner of turning
With a rising tone an uneasily-maintained assertion (like "Ahm
    Brenda-Sue?")
Into an unspecifically directed inquiry—opined
"At thee-us tahm of day, it's ohlways somehow Whensy,"
And knowing well the urgencies of busy morning when it is always
    nowsy
As well as having catalogued the nostalgias which are all so
Thensy, we could not but agree.

"Duh whole fuggin ding's godda be done by Daysday," menaced
The not-uncriminally-connected owner of the fleet of trucks,
And one continued to appreciate the openness
Of the term of the implied contract, as well as, indeed,
The grim closure by which the due date could be heard
To fall on any day, any day at all.

"Ay don't feel thet ay could be theah before Frayday," said the
    solicitor
Whose accent we deplored, but whose keen perception
Of the nature of the weekend—its hasty preparations, the rubbish
Of the unattended-to, the battle for tied position among
All the various loose ends—we could only,
No matter how inadvertent it had been, admire.

"Ull come along on Sadday," said the local who was to help
With the haying; but we could not be sure whether the mood
Of the day of his arrival would be occasioned by—or would,
Indeed, elicit—his appearance, or whether, in any case,
The prediction of that arrival was a threat or a promise.

He thought for a while—or at least appeared to think,
Perhaps in response to what we imagined *he'd* imagined to be our
    dilemma
Over the problematics of what he had so casually
Called "Sadday"—then revised his statement:
"Ull come along on Cindy," he finally announced,
Not intending to violate a sabbath however ironically
Designated but merely invoking the name of his mule.

SELECTED SHORT SUBJECTS

ON A TAG TIED TO A WINESAP
(After Moses Ibn Ezra, 11–12th cent.)

O apple with which—as first fruit of desire—
Our hunger for significance is fed:
Around your globe pale grass borders on fire,
The lovesick green pursues the blushing red.

THE ART OF FICTION

The poet who pretends to read
John Austin's essay on "Pretending"
Need never grasp its condescending
Point that pretending can't succeed.

Thus the weak-minded, headstrong youth
Private returns to his unending
Wording of fables, still pretending
Not to pretend to tell the truth.

A LINE FROM DUBELLAY

"Mère d'amour et fille de la Mer!"
Over the golden ocean waves of hair
Plunge, bright with her origin, where we
See in the water the daughter of the sea.

NOW AND THEN

Then, we were our originals, and then
We will be whatever it is to be:
Now is the moment of our mirror when
Our own seeing is part of what we see.

The middle of our moment plays both ends
Until that symmetry must be undone
And the old game of those opposing *thens*
        Now is won.

FEBRUARY MADRIGAL

Morning sun adamant and evening moon
Reigned in the warm and shaded garden
We had to leave too soon
For a world of stones;
We shiver ever after
In our cold seasons of contingent pardon,
While the wind groans.
But glittering instead
In the now nameless fallen light,
Fixed in time's frame, tonight
Eavesdropping icicles freeze up against
The warmth of our bed,
Our songs of winter, and our laughter,
Their cold hearts tensed
At what in us will die, but never harden.

THE TESSERAE (III)

71

Hard by the dry well of exhausted wealth
That brazen time with neither skill nor stealth
    Drained, we might well, before our shadows fade
Drink to the living hell of lessened health.

72

There is a last chance that our knowing takes
Before the brain, its sacred precinct, breaks:
    A final drawing in the raffle of breath,
A vacant lottery for pulled-up stakes.

73

Hope, in black tie, invited Mortality
To game away its final sovereign: see
    Bright reason squandered on the *rouge, impair*,
Les jeux sont faits. Click-click. *Les jeux sont pris.*

74

The great Hugo decreed "*Jérimadeth*"
And made a place that only rhymes beget.
    Mais en anglais, hélas! je rime à death;
(Or, till he gets what's owed, *je rime à* debt.)

75

Down corridors on that important journey,
Through parlors, carpeted and (potted-) ferny
    —His river having dried up long ago—
Charon now wheels us over on his gurney.

76

Or—[A] A muttering pain, so quietly
Inflected and oracular ... Well, [B]
  My Death—is that an answer or a question?
[C] Is B a real question? [D] Is C?

77

My pulse at midnight—something as if said,
As if to have the heart put to the head
  The question no one, without lying, can
Answer affirmatively: "*Are you dead?*"

78

The Word becomes the deed, and thereby dead;
The instant's steed rides by and in its stead
  We read its epitaph, and, having read,
The lives of gold we lead all turn to lead.

79

The Word that now I've come to die: Made clear
To light eye or to heavy, darker ear?
  Lying at night in terror of it I
Defy deaf eye. And yet if ear, I fear.

80

Sisyphus pauses; his half-bent position
Points to our own unchangeable condition:
  Seek to evade the terminus of Death?
You'll just end up in deadly Repetition.

81

Eroding gravestones, unread books, and loss
Of hearsay decompose what's left of us;
      Anent the long endurance of our names?
Anon we shall be all anonymous.

82

Being no longer made of flax or cotton,
Pages we've written on will soon be rotten,
      Just as our gesturing hands will wear away,
Just as our tones of voice will be forgotten.

83

All we have come to's that we'll all go through
It, but to no other side, the which is to
      —Finally, and unoriginally—die.
We have to do that, and have that to do.

84

I who have walked in light now make my bed
In the dark, of which there's nothing to be said.
      What radiance remains, without a me
To know it, does quite well in darkness' stead.

85

Human, and clean, and unclean disembark
Where high, yet fainter than the emptied ark,
      The arc of spectral promise gleams: the world
Will drown next time in fire before the dark.

86

My own sins taken on my own head twice
In the past, I now can offer this advice:
    Scapegoats for Azazel at least escape
Being burnt in the fires of sacrifice.

87

Somehow you feel you feel somehow the sky
Will open for an instant when you die?
    It is as open now as ever: why
Disclaim the wide, the deep, you can descry?

88

A Greek Jew who seeks wisdom in a sign,
A Christian Turk: fellows who recombine
    The follies of the East and West, the blood-
Drenched poppies sunk in bowls of fragrant wine.

89

Just past the limits of my breath, I came
Onto a place where all sounds were the same,
    High on that hill of self: rocks, caves, some trees—
Nothing there but what whispered of my name.

90

In pain, I praised my own name, hard to tell
From my Tormentor's: *Jo* /*Jah*—what the hell . . .
    Son of the afternoon, I sank to night
And bawled out "Hellelujah" as I fell.

91

Choristers to dull, turbid measures may
Fall dumbstruck in their darkness when I say,
    Out of the flaming thicket of my heart,
I am that I am in an iambic way.

92

As we are now, the long and short of it
Is our wide sorrow and our pointed wit,
    As we gaze backward, *was* seems all but endless,
Is, always shortly just about to quit.

93

With every breath I take, less of the sky
Lives; the same questions as I slowly die
    Gnaw on the world, that narrowed globe of light,
And eat away at the apple of my eye.

94

The darkening kettle strikes the blackened pot
In rage, but well before its iron is hot.
    You say my doubt slaps out thus at the world?
I know, I know. I know I know not what.

95

The figure of lean Questioning has wit
Only enough never to let him quit
    Fussing with every door—are there no locks
That any of his hundred keys will fit?

96

Doubt hops about as crickets do, in such
A manner as to keep in minimal touch
    With the hard ground in darkness. Is that stick
He carries a weapon? Or a sort of crutch?

97

(Doubt adds: "Crickets are not like me that much—
Those fiddled cadenzas, sudden leaps and such
    Are all of the high grasshopping of Hope
In the bright air with which he keeps in touch.)

98

Drops have their plenitude in time of drought,
Doubt is the seed and wonder is the sprout.
    And what comes green of all this clears the air
That is around us, that we are about.

99

The chill humanity of him who wrought
The sheer machine that severed *is* from *ought* ...
    Broken and rusted now, it's overgrown
With ghostly foliage of all he'd fought.

100

Not the pure *cogito,* nor yet the sum
Of infinite contingencies: the dumb
    Livestock of all our present moments drink
Deep from the shadowed trough of what's to come.

101

"She thinks": she and her thought are by design
Her property; "she is": by the same line
      Of reasoning, her being is her own.
But "therefore"—that's not part of her, but mine.

102

Whoever mocks the theorists of flower
Though, gives more credence to their hidden power
      To pluck, in leaves of bright discourse, the Rose
From carping hands of the fast-fading hour.

103

—But don't the rustling leaves of argument
Though acid-free, yet flake? and what once meant
      Something of meaning something fade more fast
Than "rose", "petals" and what they represent?

104

Hypotheses, lightsmiths, fall from their great
Heights slowly down on us—thus they relate
      Erring to truth, and, for a moment, shake
The constant doubts of our unsteady state.

105

Our work starts out with an initial thirst.
Then comes the fecund bit, albeit cursed
      To leave it for this pattern's broken sherd;
Then it comes forth, unfazed and unrehearsed.

106

Those quests embarked on by those More-than-Men
(Which was the last? I can't think what, or when)
    —Whether they were completed or abandoned,
No matter—won't be taken up again.

107

My wingèd chariots, my broad-sailed ships,
Once sped along on the mind's business trips;
    Now, my tired, hoarse teaching lumbers on
Under the painful cracking of these quips.

108

What future lies in formulae that treat
Our broadest terms as part of some conceit,
    "Life" as a metaphor for Everything,
And "Death" for Nothing? [this line incomplete]

IV

RIVER REMEMBERED

The rhododendrons' darkened leaves are curled
Into tight scrolls, whose dry, hermetic books
Will stay unread now, till the whitened world
Unlocks its warmth; the frozen local brooks

Muttering *sotto voce* at their own
Ice remind us of a general notion:
Some vast and abstract river's monotone
Running through land to an eventual ocean—

Not the one Wallace Stevens called "the river
Of rivers in Connecticut," inspired
Taker of water from the sea, and giver
Of meaning to the name the land acquired

(Algonquian: "long [or, tidal]-river-at")
Yet meditations on a name demand
Pulling new meanings out of an old hat:
Remembering this stream, I understand . . .

Connect . . . and Cut—those things all rivers do,
Like any kind of boundary anywhere
Linking along its length; dividing two
Banks, like the slashes in *then/now, here/there.*

And, ultimately, bridging numberless
Moments of time, those archipelagoes
That rise and fall beneath its slow caress.
All we recall is what some river knows.

One river over forty miles away
From where I gaze out at this frozen ground
I used to watch run into all the gray
And misty water of the distant Sound.

That stream, its surface flashes varying
Fragments of light like mental gems unset,
Its deeper knowledge, as from a dark spring,
Harder to grasp and harder to forget,

My memory floats over now, to stay
With scraps of past reflection from along
Its banks I knew well in a distant day
To fall into old rhythms of its song.

Gathering tidal force beyond the land,
An estuary runs up from the shore, which
Begins to narrow at New London and
Runs out of breadth at the old port of Norwich

(How the New World undoes good English names!
I know two lovely sisters: one of them's
A daughter of New London on the Thames,
The other born in England by the Thames)

—But always flowing to the ancient theme
Of time in motion and of memory—
Which, with its tidal changes, runs upstream
Carrying bits and pieces of the sea.

Her lofty ensign carrying the dread
Horst Wessel's leaky and repulsive name,
The *Eagle*'s wide topgallant wings were spread
Abroad when thirty years ago I came

For the first time to live along its bank.
Hopeful, I looked across it to the east,
The sun behind me flared up, as it sank,
In distant windows suddenly released

From ordinariness. And afterward,
Returning from a sail, we'd see the night
Awaken, as the kicker engine purred,
And look back toward the sweep of Race Rock light.

Some days, from the east bank, gobbets of floating
Gunk, that looked quite nasty, yellow, rotten,
Defaced the river's countenance, denoting
That pharmaceuticals were made at Groton.

So mirrored on the bosom of the stream
At a bad moment in our history
Lurk emblems of what happened to our dream
Of progress, health and wide prosperity:

Pollution by the fruits of our success—
The drugs that killed bacteria before
And made us fear contagion somewhat less
Now let in cancers by the cellar door.

To keep jobs open in Connecticut
(Our ends still founder in the tide of means)
We take in one another's washing. But
Groton builds missile-launching submarines,

Increasing every probability
That something, somewhere, will go wrong and—(dashes
Here are hardly needed). Who then will see
Us, and our washing, blown to dust and ashes?

—Oh see these chilling shades of foresight cast
Across memory's warm places now engage
Daylight in their transactions with the past,
And scrawl their warnings on this dimming page

Itself compounded of the ghosts of some
Forest, cut, pulped, that filled the silent land
Once, long before *homo scribens* had come,
His pens and axes held in the same hand.

And now the afternoon of early March
Gives way to dusk and splashes of a cold
Pink low in the west that overarch
The fragment of horizon I behold,

Unpromising of any warmer weather,
Between two darkened evergreens. Tonight
Too many distant rivers run together
In these last lines I've finally come to write.

VARIATIONS ON A FRAGMENT BY TRUMBULL STICKNEY

I hear a river thro' the valley wander
Whose water runs, the song alone remaining.
A rainbow stands and summer passes under,

Flowing like silence in the light of wonder.
In the near distances it is still raining
Where now the valley fills again with thunder,

Where now the river in her wide meander,
Losing at each loop what she had been gaining,
Moves into what one might as well call yonder.

The way of the dark water is to ponder
The way the light sings as of something waning.
The far-off waterfall can sound asunder

Stillness of distances, as if in blunder,
Tumbling over the rim of all explaining.
Water proves nothing, but can only maunder.

Shadows show nothing, but can only launder
The lovely land that sunset had been staining,
Long fields of which the falling light grows fonder.

Here summer stands while all its songs pass under,
A riverbank still time runs by, remaining.
I will remember rainbows as I wander.

ON NORTH ROCK

I will incline my ear
To catch the swerve of the
Silence, that is still true
    To silence itself

Even if not true of
Much of the case-laden
World. I will close my light
    Sighing to the wind

Who swishes to claim it
As one of his choirers,
One more of his choirers
    Sighing in glory

Of the world and wind, but
Without understanding.
I will open my dark
    Saying to the lyre

Something of silent light,
A singular something
Of windless dominions
    Beyond psalm or sign,

A sing-song from beyond
Clenched sign or opened psalm,
Of its own gleaming, high-
    Strung, inquiring strings.

****

Well then, a song singing
Of seeing what can be
Sung from atop North Rock,
    —Not the momently

Manifested Presence,
Scary and intimate,
Nonce, then retracted and
    Absent evermore;

Not the Feasting of the
Gods of height and light, loud
In their mountain fastness
    Clouded in fiction;

Not the vouchsafed Prospect,
At long journey's end, of
What one deserves to see
    But not to possess;

Not the late, lovely place
Like a high mountain dale,
Where a hundred naked
    Girls danced in a ring

Around a rosy and
Graceful group beside which
Stood a former fictive
    Version of oneself.

Not the windy hill that
Had finally to be
Climbed because it always
    Was there to be seen;

Not even the dumb, blank
Notional mountain I
Made a shadow-show of
   For a now-dead friend.

Not the sunny hill of
Hale and cheerful welcome
Whose own height yet darkens
   The vale of farewell.

       * * * *

Well then, a long song sung
From high above the plains
Whose low songs are only
   Of singing itself;

A song true to the lyre,
Sung of light that hums through
Its strings like sound gleaming
   Through lines on a page.

If just about the right
Height for this should be reached
At where we are now—the
   Summit of North Rock,

Where we just happened to
Be at the moment when
The hummed imperative
   Stopped nagging away

At our well-principled
Triage—then the very
Fact of that may have tuned
   The humming itself

To just the right pitch, at
Which that strumming of the
Stringings of fiction then
   Served its clear summons.

So that North Rock, undaubed
By graffiti, faded
And garish, the play of
   Myth and history,

—The place of where we **are**
Not because a star led
Us there, or a voice from
   Nowhere made us turn

Back from some primary
Journey to ascend it—
Now has become the place
   Of overstanding,

The place at of by from
Which its own tale arose
And settled, a dark and
   Invisible disk,

More reasonable than
Any laws of limit
Laid down by the line of
   Any horizon.

       * * * *

Whalley and Dixwell and
Goffe, they sat on West Rock
Whacking off; said Dixwell
   To Whalley, "We can't

Do this daily: the wind
Up here's making me cough."
She and I sat on East
   Rock in the car and

Looked out over the sad
Small city's scattering
Of lights and distant dark
   Water and thought of

Separate things, there in
Our bodies, separate
Mindfull bodies, that had
   Not yet touched nor sought

To become each other
Yet, but high on East Rock
Trembled in the dark of
   The late April air.

Giggled histories of
Regicides on the lam,
Souvenirs of sighing
   Longings of ago—

On North Rock at night, song
Is more cold and more bright
Than on those eternal
   But contending hills;

More light and more bold than
The old chants of desire
And the chronicles of
   Kings and their killers

Is the lovely chant, the
Ever American
Chant, the veriest chant,
   The song of itself.

* * * *

The sun, assembling his
West-Östlicher Divan
Updates all the oldest
   Bright observations;

The meandering moon,
With her book of silver
Vocalises turns these
   High rocks to dark stone.

But through the cold, noble
Prose of the northern dark
Wind the threads of thought, plucked
   By the loud high wind,

The wind more elevate,
In whose thrummings we hear
All our common story
   At its greatest height,

In its splendid mummings
The eternal turning
Of the constancies, the
   Fancy truth of things.

* * * *

South Rock, sunup and down:
The Hills that face each other
Acknowledge what comes and
   Goes and comes and goes,

Rock to reddening rock
Partaking of the stuff
Of these arrivals and
    Departures, taking

Part in all these shows, the
Left hand barely knowing
What earlier the right
    Hand had been doing,

Rock to rock darkening
Or paling at noon hides
In its waving banter
    Of greeting (*"Hi, there,*

Other Rock!) jealousies
One might expect, early
And late recipients
    Of light each in doubt

About which of them is
Better off, when they have
No rivals there above
    The benighted plain.

None of that stuff here on
Our place that is beyond
That kind of height, unlit
    By that kind of light.

In this unblinding night
We shall lie here and look
Skyward between the sparse
    Stars and see patterns

That diagram our loves
Lasting beyond desires,
Our very seeing, and
    Our saying itself,

Our dark saying opened
To the lyre of night
Light, to the moment of
    Gleaming commandment.

         * * * *

One doesn't come up here
At dawn or even worse
At sunset, when the light
    Can never be quite

What we'd want, let alone
What we'd need, let alone
Whatever . . . I have no
    Wish now to witness

The undergoing of
The evening lands (as if
They were some enduring
    Kind of punishment)

By our senses of space,
The sight of our daylight
Dying in its own blood
    Splashed in the high air.

And as for the light that
Prophesies imminent
Sunrise, it is cheap stuff
    (Anything would look

Impressive after all
That not-being-able-
To see anything) it
   Is such easy stuff.

         ＊ ＊ ＊

We must take it hard, though;
And it is too late for
Working through to the time
   When we laze with all

The ease we feel we have
Earned and gaze at some blue
Body of water that
   Figures our desire

(Being so late that we
Can't be certain just how
Late it really is, it
   Is too late for that);

Thus it is high time to
Find oneself at the right
High place and take up the
   Heavy task of what

It means, what it all means,
Rather than carrying
On, for what to *do* then
   —Dancing in joy or

Pain, shouting to what will
Ever be unhearing,
Trembling in the cold,
   Descending with some

Souvenir—is lightness,
An old lightness; now for
Us the standing here, for
   Us the grace of weight.

         ＊ ＊ ＊

Tales tolled out in the high
Bells of wind, low whispers
In the face of darkness,
   All now hushed, now all

Hushed. Interestingness
And hope for joy and joy
Of hope hushed now, wisdoms
   Amid promises hushed,

Utterly hushed as if
They were celebrating
In all those triumphant
   Diminuendos

The great night itself, which
Turned over, rolled slowly
Over and revealed for
   A thoughtful moment

A flash of the nothing
They had been awaiting,
Which, reflected in night's
   Mirror, is the Dark.

Then there would be substance
Too new yet to have cast
Past shadows, then could be
   Heard not-yet-told tales.

THE SEE-SAW

"Of the remedies acting primarily on the body, the see-saw especially has proved efficacious, especially with raving lunatics. The see-saw movement induces giddiness in the patient and loosens his fixed idea."

G. W. F. HEGEL, Zusatz to section 408 of the *Encyclopedia of the Philosophical Sciences* (tr. A. V. Miller)

Margery daw.
And up she went as I went down
And up she went and then I saw
The hair between her legs was brown.

Hold the handle with just your thumbs
And flap your fingers. Smile and frown
And giggle and sigh . . . we know what comes
Up must come down.

Up! and the end of the tip of me thrills:
Now I see over
The playground fence to the lovely hills,
The shadowy dales, the meadows of clover.

Down! and I bump . . . a hardened cough . . .
Against the place where I have a tail
(Do I have a tail? If I do, then they'll
Cut it all off.)

Mechanical Operations of
The Spirit oscillate between
The high of hate, the low of love,
As we have seen;

As we have sawn
So shall we rip, this way and that
Way, up and down, and my peace has gone
Off to war in a funny hat.

Two bolts on the handle dream of me
Like eyes (those very eyes I see
Saw something dirty they did to you,
Margery Doo)

A fulcrum with an idée fixe
(Hear how it creaks!)
Won't be shaken, *Balance is all.*
I'm unbalanced, a head-shaped ball.

Margery Dall:
I'd fill her up but my thing's too small,
She'd fill me down with her legs apart.
Every stopper gives me a start.

Here I come and she goes there,
Each of us President of the Air,
Slave of the Ground.
It's square that makes the world go round.

Toes just touch the ground, she and I,
Gravel and sky,
Balanced now in the midst of flight
Listen for yesterday, wait for night.

Something bad back-and-forth was there
Under Grandmother's rocking chair,
With his hanging weights and his swinging cock,
Grandfather Clock

Punishes Pa,
Ravishes Ma, and ticks the tock
Of now and then and the Time they mock.
Und ich bin hier und Margery da.

And she goes low and I go high
By an inexorable law:
See me be born? I saw Margery die,
Margery Daw.

See saw.

My wooden slope can't get to sleep,
The peaks are sunken the moon down deep,
The desert damp and the sea sere
Margery Dear
I'm here there, and you're there here.
Margery Day,
Sold her old bed to lie on straw
To die on straw on the Days of Awe;
Margery Daw on the Days of Play
Goes up and down in the same old way

Und ich bin hier und Margery da
Tra la la la.

Out and down and up and back,
All comes on now faster and faster
When will I rest? and when will Jack
"Have a new master?"

I watch the light by which I see
Saw away at my wooden head,
Living or dead?
I haven't been told and I'll never be.

Who is it calls us home from play?
That nurse of darkness with Nothing to say.
One last up and down. And then
Never again.

THE TESSERAE (IV)

109

These lines, these bits and pieces, each a token
Of ruined method, of "a knowledge broken,"
      Inaudible, leave traces when they pass
As if the fragments of our speech had spoken.

110

And those who husbanded the amber wine,
And those who splashed it into flagons, sign
      The same receipt, as the one Spirit Shoppe
Delivers what's distilled from the divine.

111

Blind to injustice, what can you stand *for*,
Rusted and twisted your slow sword, and your
      Balance with its twin pans shot through with holes?
Astraea was a virgin. You're a whore.

112

High public office, for Sam, Joe and Bill
(Our leaders) yields the same old prizes still:
      The minor thrill of public song-and-dance
A hand in someone's pants, or in the till.

113

The Muse?—It's not the strange gods, but the cheap
Ones she goes whoring after; yet we keep
      Her seriously chaste with knowing laughter,
Tickling her soul so she won't fall asleep.

114

"Seek not in the long *suk* for more than cant,"
Hakim warned, "nor fruit on the flowering plant."
    False coin still rings true in the marketplace...
(*"A parnus oyf Parnassus?"* shrugged my aunt).

115

My sight blurs. "Wisdom"—in the transcribed word
Ḥaḥma—turns into *"hoḳum"* when interred
    In the firm ground of modern English: which—
Old wisdom or our speech—is more absurd?

116

Avoid all Angel Food: eat marble cake—
Only without the idiots who take
    Us to task for it, could we then abandon
Complication for complication's sake.

117

Faber est suae quisque fortunae (read:
"We are the shapers of our fates") Indeed?
    That feared and courted strumpet Fortune smiles,
Parcelling us out the tools she feels we need.

118

Our home is burning while logicians fiddle:
The stately Law of the Excluded Middle
    Must bow out now, and leave us room to breathe
Between the mad coals and the hissing griddle.

119

Whose ugly effigy hangs from the rafter—
The crafty artist or the artsy crafter?
  Which of them made it? In whose image was
It fashioned? Distant Beauty dissolved in laughter.

120

Like thin, new wines that the bad vintners weep
That sour the heart and put one's wits to sleep,
  The shrill chants of the hour soon go bad;
Songs of the lion and the lizard keep.

121

(Rustum with his unrusting sword could "cause
The air to weep." Firdawsi gives us pause,
  Who first caused Rustum, with his trusty pen
And set the high winds roaring in applause.)

122

The escalator of surprise today
Only takes you to ladies' lounjeray,
  But in the steady basement yard-goods still
Can fly like words with wings and things to say.

123

April will make a difference, come what may,
To our chilled hearts still gripped by Yesterday,
  Till May push on with all its might and main,
Showering us with flowers on its way.

124

Répète in French can also mean "rehearse"
As if for some past event, lovely, or (worse)
        Terminal. English repetition, all
Aftermath, implies just the reverse.

125

Or put another way: diminishing
Returns are those to which we must not cling,
        Time's small, alarming bells begin to ring
The end of this—if not of every—thing.

126

The reaping whirlwind sows its rows of night
Thoughts yet, archaic, innocent and trite
        Fears of the rage of human, all too human
Nature, twisting, capricious in its might.

127

Mild wind in late, light blossoms cannot stem
The fevered pulse of this offbeat mayhem,
        Hard crows in caucus here, as if mid-spring
Had never come to soften even them.

128

The present moment scribbles, after much heated
Argument, at its soon-to-be-completed
        A Prolegomenon to Any Future,
In which the central questions will be treated.

129

Early for breakfast laughing sunlight brought
A dish of feelings, delicate, fresh-caught;
    Now I munch on leftovers of my life
In midnight silences, cold food for thought.

130

Now, in the morning light, a kind of summing
Up of silences, while time keeps humming,
    Humming, going about its only business.
Dying's a process. Death is unbecoming.

131

The lesson for today will be Today;
Once read, the sermon on it, come what may,
    Becomes part of the text itself, nor cares
That nothing's left to which, with which, to pray.

132

Thought brings me to the barely-wakened brink
Of this still pool. My eyes will only drink
    Of mirroring, my fear not being that
I think I dream, but that I dream I think.

133

The gaming-tables now have sunk to slumber;
Green baize gives way to ochre and to umber;
    Euchre and ombre both give way to poker,
Its joker, and its wild cards without number.

134

The ambers of this afternoon will creep
Across the carpet, where their shadows seep
      Into the pool of its own dark grey fur
In which one of my kittens lies asleep.

135

Wearied from having wandered far, the heart
At home by its loud-purring hearth will start
      Up again at the memory of great
Cities in homelands half a world apart.

136

The wind soars through the waiting air and clears
Some loosened branch. A sharp crack. No one hears
      But two cats: Jane listens with her whole body,
Motionless Pansy, just with her gray ears.

137

All cats are gray at midnight, when the moon
Shines or when it doesn't, though morning soon
      Puts a stop to all that, until each cat's
Too singularly like itself at noon.

138

Pair and square alike cry out for more,
As if oddness were all they could adore
      Where had those first two lines been pointing to?
Here? What all four had all been headed for?

139

My *kuzà nàmeh* ("Song of Pots") begins
To end. Each vessel on its wheel now spins
　　　Backward: the maker's name—MAYYAHK RAMO—
Rebukes me for my efforts, for my sins.

140

Clay beads, glass, quartz, the odd enameled thing,
Gouts of garnet, a sapphire, could bring
　　　Amusing kinds of brightness to this strand.
I've few beads left, I'm running out of string.

141

Tired now, by candlelight and in the grip
Of much undoing to be done, we strip
　　　Away at varnish, burn old wills and deeds,
As in our work we sew, so shall we rip.

142

We scatter over caskets many trite
Cut flowers, lovely, variegated, bright,
　　　And brief of life as we; and short poems, too,
Ever-enduring as eternal night.

143

Where, Lo, the maker of the tents had caught
This beast, four-footed, in a noose of thought,
　　　I peered through pointed thorns among the Old
Roses still growing, and I pulled it taut.

144

I've painted, in high light, with colors of
Shadows cast by the dark itself, in love
  With shows of blackness. May I play with light
When covering darkness fits me like a glove.

NOTES

AN OLD FASHIONED-SONG   *Nous n'irons plus au bois / Les lauriers sont coupé* (We'll go no more to the woods / The laurels have been cut down)—from a French children's round-dance.

AN OLD COUNTING-GAME   to the pattern of a song, *Echad mi yodeyah?,* (Who knows One?) sung after the Passover Seder.

MAKING NOTHING HAPPEN   *Tohu u bohu,* usually translated *without form and void* in Genesis 1.1.

COLORED ILLUSTRATION, TIPPED IN   In children's books, a few half-tone or colored plates on coated paper used to be tipped in among the ordinary pages of text. I am thinking here of those by painters like N.C. Wyeth or Howard Pyle.

BREAD-AND-BUTTER!   In my childhood, two people walking along and holding hands would each say this if some intervening obstacle caused them temporarily to break their grasp.

10/18/29   The date of the author's birth speaks.

FROM OUT OF THE BLACK   "I bowed down . . . long" See Pslam 38.6.

INTO THE BLACK   See Genesis 15.5.

RIVER REMEMBERED   The square-rigged *Eagle,* a training ship of the U.S. Coast Guard Academy in New London, was originally built in Germany and named for the martyred Nazi thug Horst Wessel.

ON NORTH ROCK   Whereas "North Rock" and "South Rock" are mythological heights, East Rock and West Rock are prominent, isolated hills on either side of New Haven, Connecticut. The latter of these is associated with the three judges, John Dixwell, Edward Whalley and William Goffe, who condemned Charles I to death, and who fled to the Colonies at the Restoration. Two of them hid out on top of it, aided by the third who visited them there. "I will open my dark saying to the lyre": Psalm 49.5. The *West-Östlicher Divan* was Goethe's great collection based on his responses to Persian poetry.

THE SEE-SAW   Running through my head as I considered the ridiculousness of the passage from Hegel was the Mother Goose rhyme: "See-saw / Margery

Daw / Jack shall have a new master. / He must have but a penny a day / Because he can't go any faster." This meant more to me than the obvious problem with Hegel's notion posed by see-sawing itself as a fixed idea.

THE TESSERAE:

[4] "Silent beside . . . sea": *bê d'akéon para thina poluphloisboio thalassês* (*Iliad* I.34).

[6] "Old pictures of Apollo": like the engraving of an Apollo by Rosso Fiorentino with the inscription *OMNA QUI VIDEO PER QUEM VIDET MONIA TELLUS.*

[7] "Thales had to say": at least, according to Diogenes Laertius.

[23] "*et iam summa procul villarum culmina fumantmaioresque cadunt altis de montibus umbrae*" Virgil, Eclogue I, 82–3.

[31] "knowing Wittengenstein": *Zettel*, #216.

[32] The name of the Biblical prophetess Deborah means "bee" in Hebrew.

[39] Lying in hiding here is the six-line stanza rhyming *x* / *here* / *x* / *clear* / *dry* / *by*.

[59] See H. L. Ginzberg, *The Legends of the Jews*, I, 66.

[61] "The Talmud says": *Pirke Aboth*, 4.13.

[74] In his celebrated "*Booz endormi*", Victor Hugo, unable otherwise to find a necessary rhyme, invented the notional North-Semitic sounding place-name, "I-am-rhyming-on-*deth*".

[86] "Scapegoats for Azazel": Leviticus 16:8–10.

[88] "For the Jews require a sign, and the Greeks seek after wisdom" I Corinthians 1.22.

[89] Acrostic.

[96] See Michelangelo's verse, Girardi 65, #10.

[97] Added in response to a doubting question by Stanley Cavell.

[109] "a knowledge broken" I seem to remember this as a phrase of Bacon's.

[114] *hakim* is a physician; *a parnus* is Yiddish for making a living, a job.

[115] There is no etymological connection I know of between Hebrew *hahma* (="wisdom") and our modern slang word, although Arabic *hakim* (see above) is indeed cognate with it.

[117] "Each man is the smith of his own fortune"—Appius Claudius Caecus, quoted by Sallust.

[121] Said of Rustum in the *Shah-Nameh*, (the "Epic of Kings") of Firdawsi.

[139] This and number 143 by way of acknowledgment. The *kuzà nàmeh* is a designated section of Omar Khayyam's *Rubaiyat* in which pots speak as people.

John Hollander's first book of poems, A CRACKLING OF THORNS, *was chosen by W. H. Auden as the 1958 volume in the Yale Series of Younger Poets;* MOVIE-GOING AND OTHER POEMS *appeared in 1962,* VISIONS FROM THE RAMBLE *in 1965,* TYPES OF SHAPE *in 1969,* THE NIGHT MIRROR *in 1971,* TALES TOLD OF THE FATHERS *in 1975,* REFLECTIONS ON ESPIONAGE *in 1976,* SPECTRAL EMANATIONS *in 1978,* BLUE WINE *in 1979,* POWERS OF THIRTEEN *in 1983 and* IN TIME AND PLACE *in 1986. He has written four books of criticism,* THE UNTUNING OF THE SKY, VISION AND RESONANCE, RHYME'S REASON *and* THE FIGURE OF ECHO *and edited both* THE LAUREL BEN JONSON *and, with Harold Bloom,* THE WIND AND THE RAIN, *an anthology of verse for young people, an anthology of contemporary poetry,* POEMS OF OUR MOMENT *and was a co-editor of* THE OXFORD ANTHOLOGY OF ENGLISH LITERATURE. *He is the editor (with Anthony Hecht, with whom he shared the Bollingen Prize in Poetry in 1963) of* JIGGERY-POKERY: A COMPENDIUM OF DOUBLE DACTYLS. *Mr. Hollander attended Columbia and Indiana Universities, was a junior fellow of the Society of Fellows of Harvard University, and taught at Connecticut College and Yale, and was Professor of English at Hunter College and the Graduate Center,* CUNY. *He is currently A. Bartlett Giamatti Professor of English at Yale. In 1990 he was made a Fellow of the MacArthur Foundation. A companion volume to this one,* SELECTED POETRY, *is issued simultaneously.*

A NOTE ON THE TYPE

This book was set on the Linotype in Granjon, a type named
in compliment to Robert Granjon but neither a copy of a classic
face nor an entirely original creation. George W. Jones based
his designs on the type used by Claude Garamond (c. 1480–
1561) in his beautiful French books. Granjon more closely
resembles Garamond's own type than does any of the various
modern types that bear his name.

Robert Granjon began his career as type cutter in 1523. The
boldest and most original designer of his time, he was one of
the first to practice the trade of type founder apart from that
of printer. Between 1557 and 1562 Granjon printed about
twenty books in types designed by himself, following, after
the fashion, the cursive handwriting of the time. These types,
usually known as *caractères de civilité*, he himself called *lettres
françaises*, as especially appropriate to his own country.

*Composition and printing by Heritage Printers, Inc.,
Charlotte, North Carolina
Binding by Kingsport Press, Kingsport, Tennessee
Designed by Harry Ford*